The D-String Book for Viola

by Cassia Harvey

CHP338

©2018 by C. Harvey Publications All Rights Reserved.

www.charveypublications.com

Playing the D string

Cassia Harvey

Playing the D string with "Mississippi Hot Dog"

©2018 C. Harvey Publications All Rights Reserved.

Writing the Note "D"

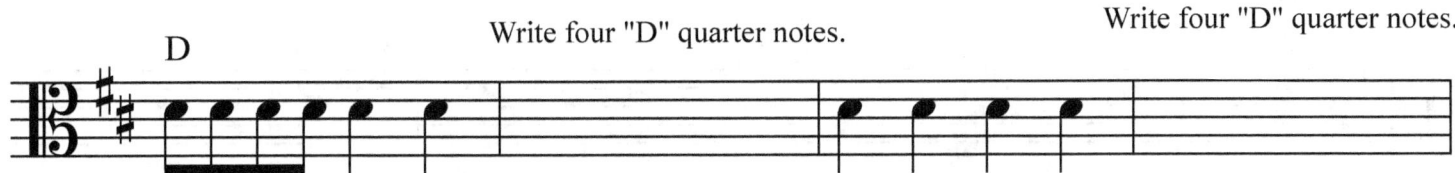

Rhythm Review

First Finger "E" on the D String

Rhythms with D and E

The D-String Book for Viola

D string March

Reviewing the Note "E"

©2018 C. Harvey Publications All Rights Reserved.

Learning Second Finger "F#"

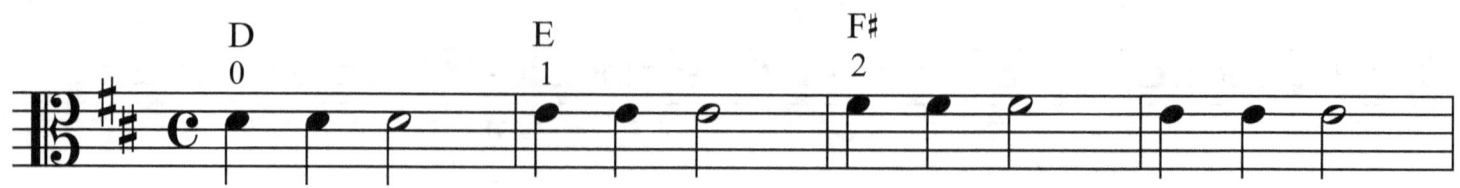

Mary Had a Little Lamb

Hot Cross Buns with Variations

Squashed 'Shortning Bread'

American Folk Tune

©2018 C. Harvey Publications All Rights Reserved.

Note-Name Study #1

D E D E

F# E F# E

D E F# E

D F# E D

Note-Name Study #2

F# D E F#

E D E D

F# D E F#

E F# E D

The Coordination Song

©2018 C. Harvey Publications All Rights Reserved.

Running To the Waves

Jellyfish

Finger Trainer

Dolphin Song

Make your bows as smooth as possible.

Skipping to Second Finger

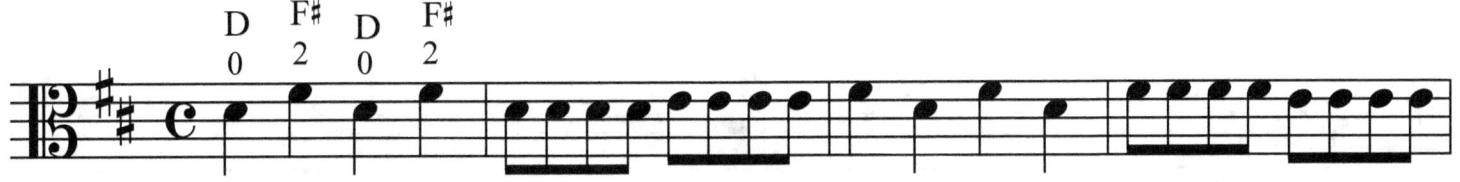

Straight to the Moon

French Folk Song

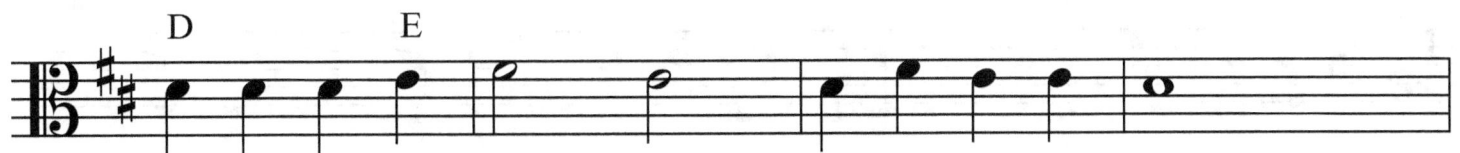

©2018 C. Harvey Publications All Rights Reserved.

Taking a Boat Ride

Seasick

©2018 C. Harvey Publications All Rights Reserved.

Learning 3rd Finger "G"

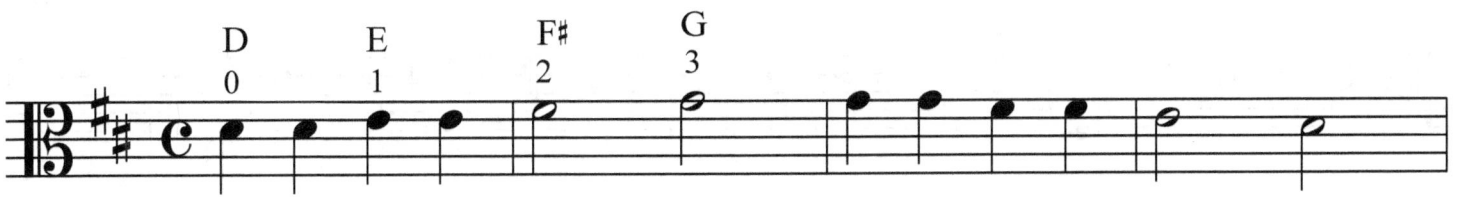

Rhythm With the New Note "G"

Searching for Pennies in the Sand

The Skipping Study

©2018 C. Harvey Publications All Rights Reserved.

The D-String Book for Viola

The Scale Workout

Little French Song

D String Exercise

Danish Contredans

The D-String Book for Viola

The Sandal Song

Folk Song

Counting Exercise

©2018 C. Harvey Publications All Rights Reserved.

Wild Horse Rhythm Training

Here, a quarter note gets 2 counts!

The Wild Horses

©2018 C. Harvey Publications All Rights Reserved.

The D-String Book for Viola

The Seaweed Song

Fiddle Tune

©2018 C. Harvey Publications All Rights Reserved.

Learning 4th Finger "A"

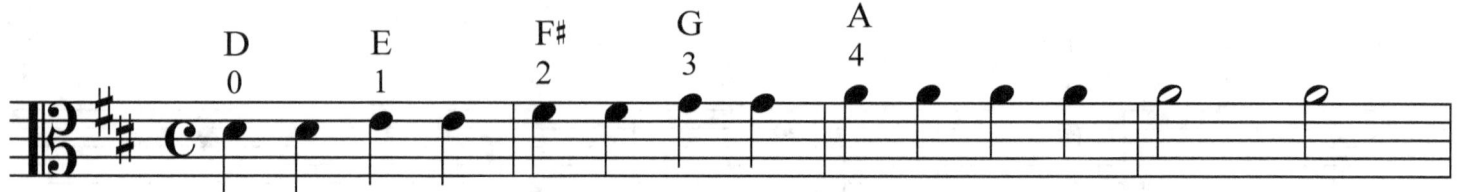

John Peel

English Folk Song

©2018 C. Harvey Publications All Rights Reserved.

The D-String Book for Viola

Using "A"

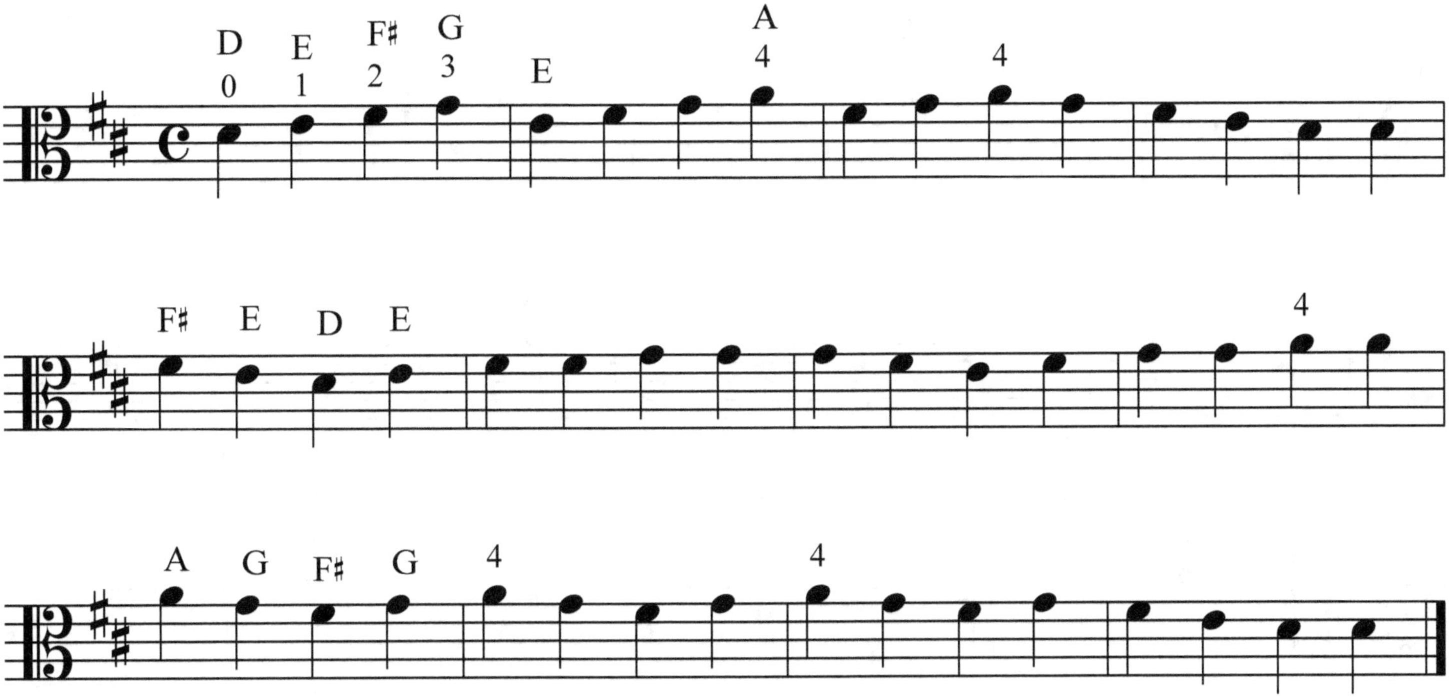

Mozart's Sonata Theme

Skipping Exercise

Shoemaker's Dance

Danish Folk Song

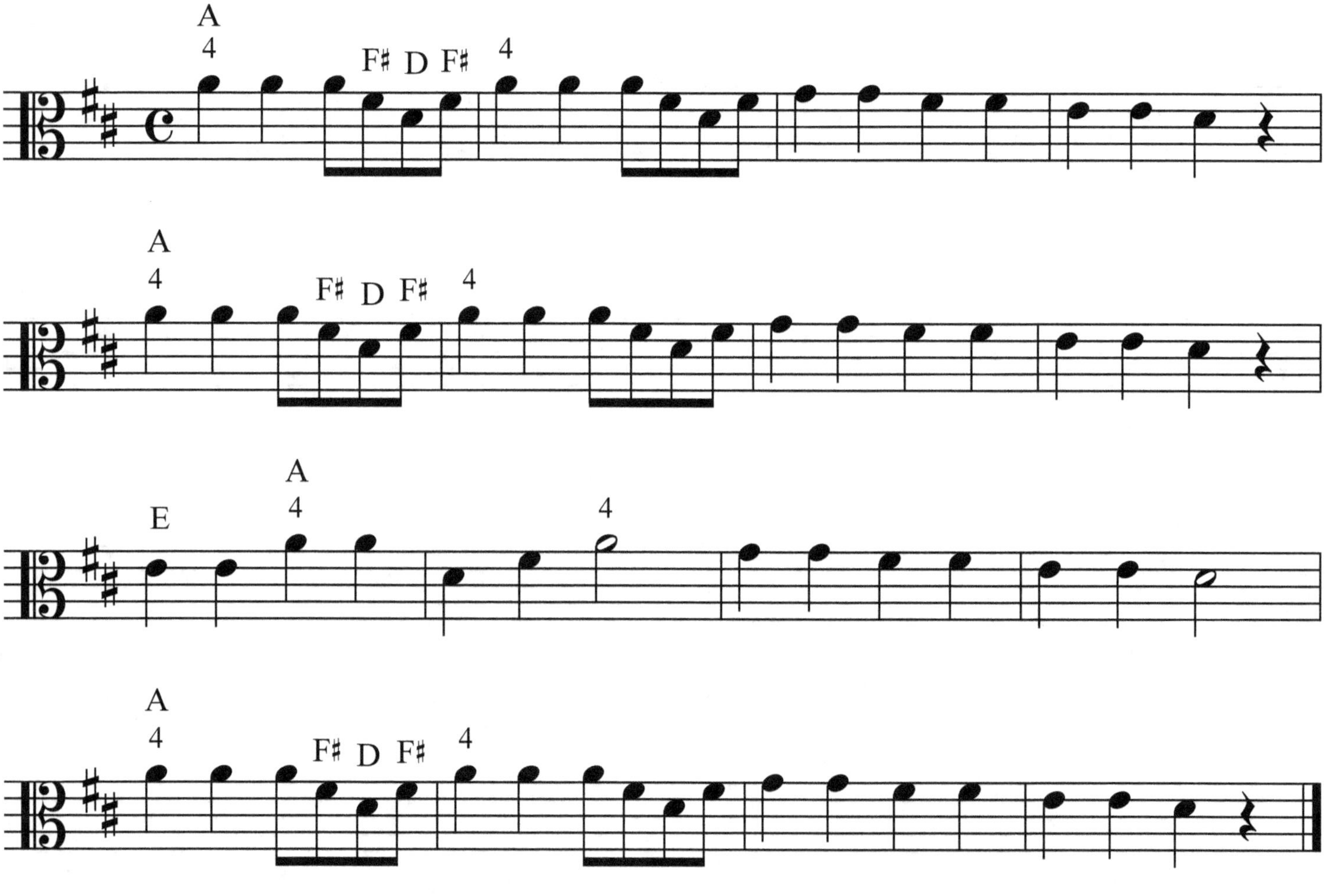

The D-String Book for Viola

More Counting in 6/8

23

Here, a quarter note gets 2 counts!

Humpty Dumpty

English Folk Song

©2018 C. Harvey Publications All Rights Reserved.

The Speed Exercise

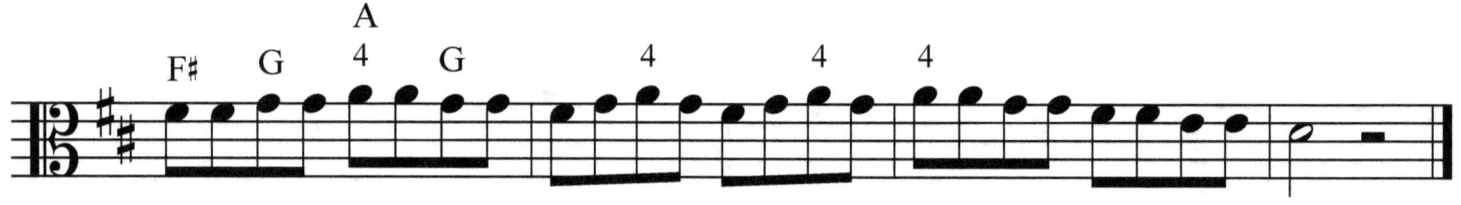

Folk Lullaby

German Folk Song

The D-String Book for Viola

Finger Twister

The Galloping Pony

American Folk Song

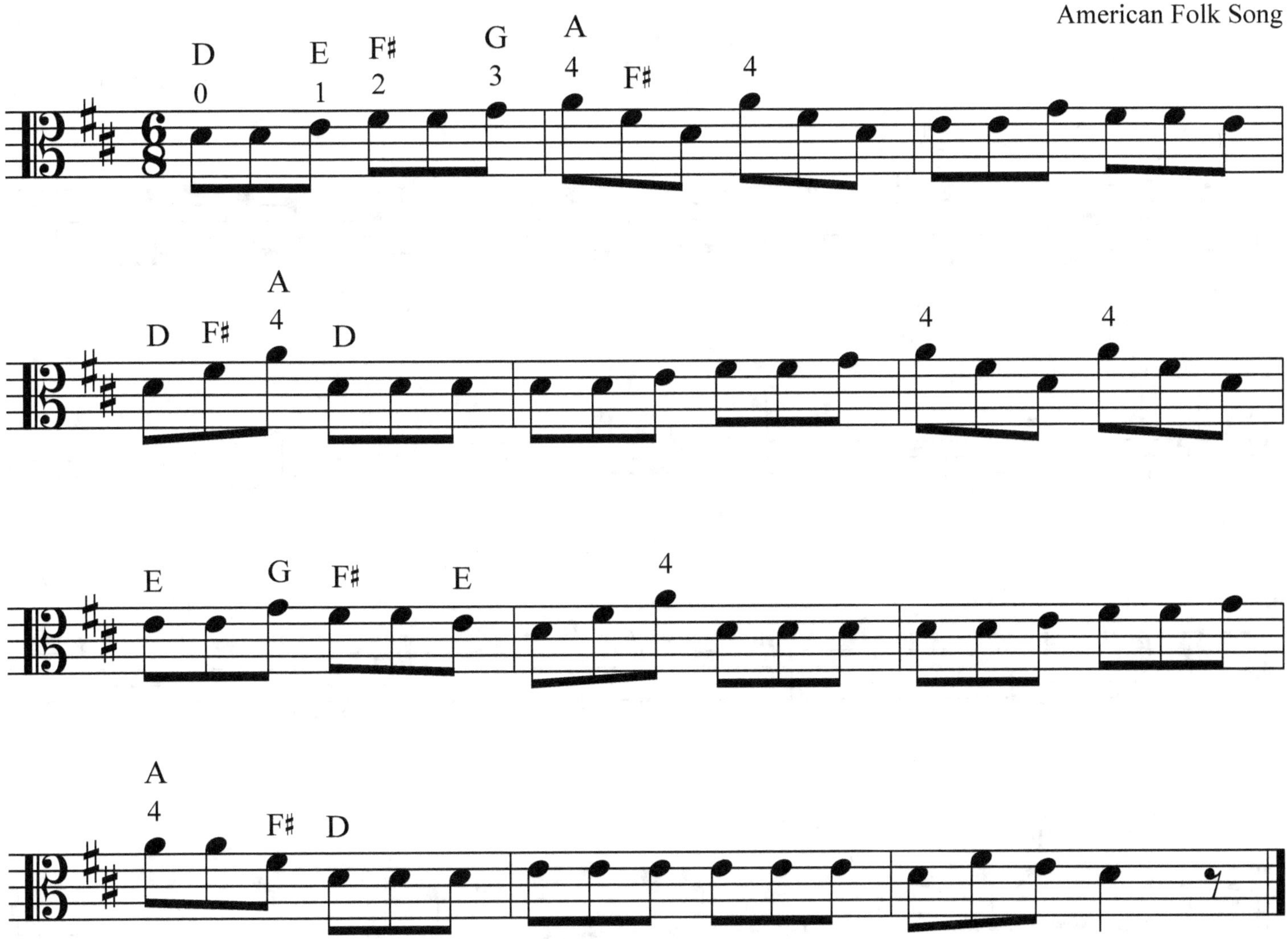

©2018 C. Harvey Publications All Rights Reserved.

Warm-Up #1

Little Sally Waters
English Folk Song

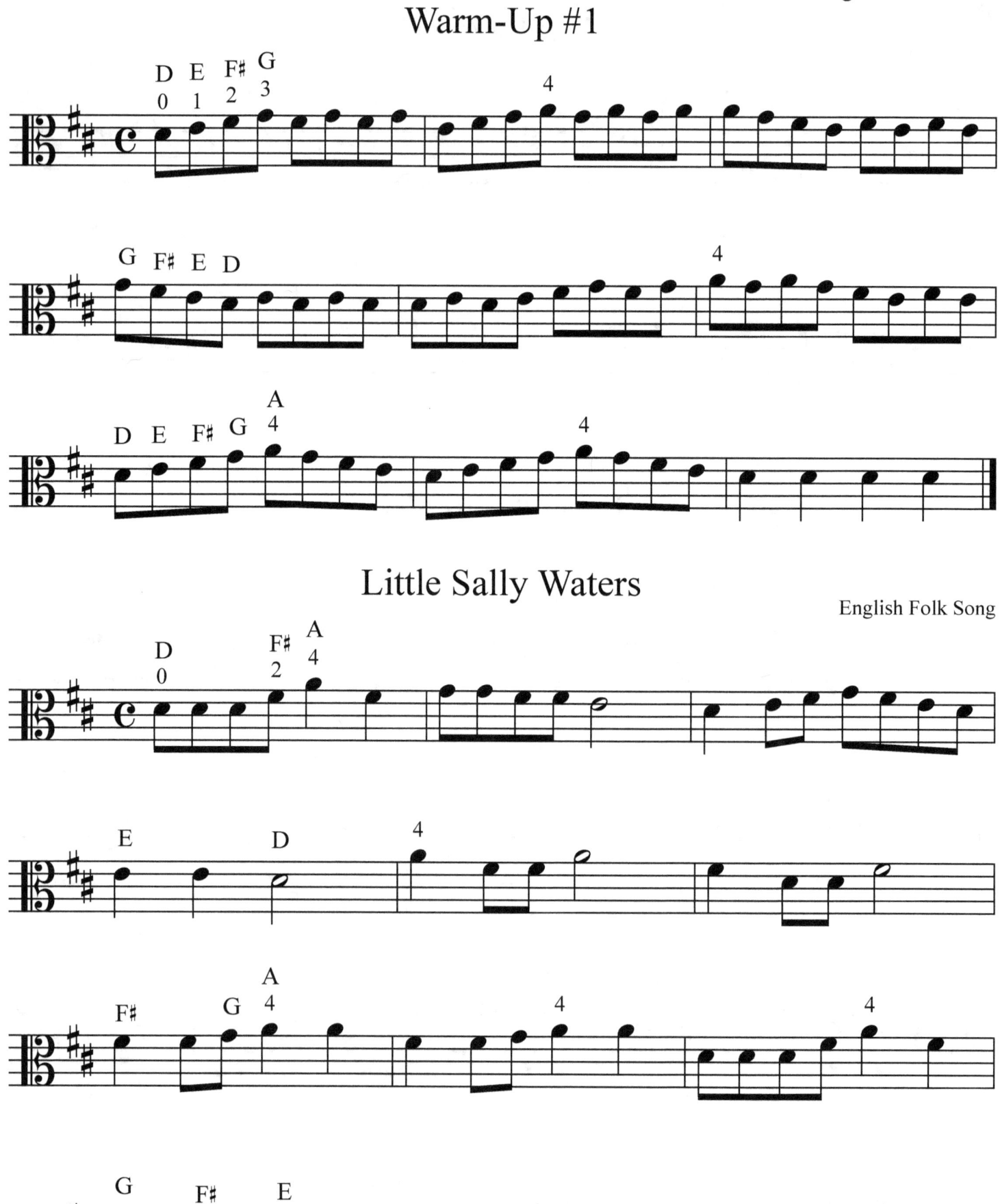

Note Review

Yankee Doodle

American Folk Song

available from **www.charveypublications.com**: CHP251

Double Stop Beginnings for the Viola, Book One

Double Stop Beginnings for the Viola, Book One

Part 1

Cassia Harvey

©2014 C. Harvey Publications All Rights Reserved.

www.ingramcontent.com/pod-product-compliance
Lightning Source LLC
Chambersburg PA
CBHW051431070526
44584CB00023B/3679